2018.

CANIM,

I'm so happy to finally be able to share this with you. My absolute favourite human. May these words move you, & inspire you to speak power to your own truth.

I love you madly!!

Basak
xo

2018.

CAHIM,

I'm so happy to finally
is able to share this
with you. My absolute
favourite human.
May these words
move you, & inspire
you to speak your
to you own truth.

I love you madly!!

Renak
xo

HOMECOMING

A Poetry Collection.

BASAK ERTEN

HOMECOMING

© 2018, Basak Erten
ISBN: 9781980534655
Self-published
info@homecoming.com
All rights reserved.

No part of this publication may be reproduced, stored in
a retrieval system, stored in a database and
/or published in any form or by any means, electronic,
mechanical, photocopying, recording or otherwise,
without the prior written permission of the publisher.

We travel, some of us forever, to seek other states, other lives, other souls.

Anaïs Nin

CONTENTS

PREFACE [1]

[I]
the LAND [3]

[II]
the DROUGHT [31]

[III]
the SPRING [67]

[IV]
the BLOOM [97]

For my Baba, without whom I would not be:

*I love you entirely.
I love you eternally.*

HOMECOMING

PREFACE

*This is my attempt at owning my story.
Of standing, firmly in my truth.
If you're reading this.
This is my carving,
This is me carving.
Ink as scalpel.
Pain as anecdote.
To immortalise,
The living of trajectories.
To capture,
The feeling process
That is,
That has become, my life.
I have laid down,
The edges and the grooves,
I have traded in,
Truth, for freedom.
Crafted something in spite of
The harsh seasons
Given into something
Because of,
The morning dew.*

*May you find strength in these pages, also.
May you give yourself the grace of feeling, also.
Even for that which you cannot say-out-loud.
Especially for that which you cannot say-out-loud.
May you,
Bloom all the way home,
To yourself,
Also.*

HOMECOMING

[I] the LAND

HOMECOMING

Something about the essence of a woman,
All soft skin and brilliant resolve.
Made up of cocoa butter and conviction.
She is both, full breast and sharp tongue.
Intriguing country, and native motherland.

Glory,
Glory,
Glory.

It is a pleasure to know you.
It is an honour to be of you.

- Homeland

Boadicea and Her Daughters

It was in loss,
not in love,
That your life's purpose found you.
May I too,
rise,
so spectacularly,
even after my demons have had their way.

Darling, don't you realise,
You
Have been waiting for, you.
Your whole life?

- Soulmate

HOMECOMING

All that you have been gifted,
The wisdom,
The feeling,
The intuition.
It stems from,
The struggle.

It took me twenty something years to realise this.
It took me twenty something years
to kneel,
before,
my demons.
and thank them.

(Profusely).

- Grateful

HOMECOMING

There is such conviction in this stance,
such comfort in this skin,
such *charm* in this walk.
Even if I have to claw my way back into remembering.

I am a constellation endlessly unfolding unto myself.
I am a galaxy to be felt,
I am
an experience,
all my own.

- For Those That Must Be Lived, To Be Felt.

How to conceptualise
The scope of your mind,
The shine in your eyes,
The breadth of your love.
My oh my.

Demi-God in feminine flesh:
How I have spent a lifetime
Searching for you.

- Reflections

HOMECOMING

I am full woman,
moon woman,
trying to make whole
half hearts.
Trying to feed,
hungry eyes.
Flesh as offering,
skin as currency.
a secret plea escapes between
my lips.
See more.
My last coherent thought,
before I'm pulled under.
Please,
see more.

- Depth

You are nothing but lips.
Big juicy pears drooping from the top of your chin.
So seductively,
How could I not stare?
So overtly,
It's partly embarrassing.
Your feminine brings out within me, a lust I cannot contain.

As if you choose to be seen as nothing but lips.
Because the strength of your mind, or the will of your spirit are not sexy enough.
So you paint those lips, blood red.
And you allow yourself to be just, red lips.
In the hope that the beholder may someday
See so much more
In you
Then just
The sum
Of
Your parts.

- Reductions

In the Presence of the Divine

He told me,
I was pure muscle.
Like the women that came before me,
Made in furnaces, bound and wrought with iron clad steel.
I feel my ancestors in my bones.
Their breath aligns my every move.
Living vicariously; they are hard shell encased in soft sentimentality.
They live just above my rib cage,
Backbone that stretches the span of a century.
Their presence a palpable entity; strength riddled with the juice of a thousand pomegranates.
Dripping with honey, their eyes do not give away
The battles that have been waged;
The battles that have been won.

How do you manage to be both crackling whip and dissembling smile?
The kind to stop a legion of men in their tracks.
Shaping even the most hardened of hearts, in your own image.
How do you manage to be both the pulp and the fruit?
Though you've been chewed up and spat out.
Relentlessly so,
Your resilience never wavers,
Your resilience never wavered.

HOMECOMING

You were birthed, fists clenched tight into this world.
Shedding skin like the stripping of pine.
You devoured the pain in its entirety;
Always searching for segments of truth,
Like the tearing of iridescent clementines.
Knees bent, head bowed unto yourself
It is within you, you found,
The Moses, the Jesus, and the Abraham.
Parted the seas with the force of your femininity.
Celestial whole; your very thoughts become physical manifestations.
With one gaze. With that gaze.
You cultivate life through your fingertips,
You create life through your touch.

Simultaneously so,
You are both the cocoon wrapped in silk and the rose petal in full blossom.

If I ever learn to smooth my edges,
Without losing my edge.

I too may stand to be,
Half of the women
That exist, within me.

Cleo

You, with your half moon gaze,
Well-versed in the art of rapture.
Always knowing how to leave your imprint.
A thief in the night.
You, with your inviting eyes
You, the one who never knew how to stay.

Comfort is sought
in the contours
of dark,
glistening skin.

- Confessions

HOMECOMING

On the nights that
He takes you into his embrace,
With my name on his lips.
Do not turn away.
Instead,
Explore the continents along his back
The smooth ridges and sharp curves I'm too far to touch.

On the nights that,
He pulls you into his embrace,
With my perfume lingering in his lungs.
Do not turn away.
Instead,
Fondle the edges of his mouth,
All his sweet nothings live there.

On the nights that,
The passion unfurls
And you finally believe
He.Is.All.Your.Own.
Just know,
He is racing across cities in his mind.
Tasting me,
In the warmth of you.

- Soul Ties

HOMECOMING

I wish I could touch you but
Home is lukewarm now.
Besides, out of reach is
The only thing we know.
It's the only thing we've ever known.

- A Tragedy In Five Lines

HOMECOMING

Even after all these years.
Your name, with it's Aramaic origins,
Swishes like iron and blood as they gurgle it in their mouth;

As they attack it mercilessly, with their tongues.

It serves to remind you,
You are still considered that-which-is-other,
In the very city which-you-call-home.

- Pronunciation

Columbus

I am not your taste of something foreign,
I am not your taste of something sweet.
You have not sailed the depths of the seven oceans
Nor explored the breadth of the five continents
By touching the crevices of my contours.

Though you must kneel at my altar,
I am not your sip at the holy chalice,
Nor, your crowning hallelujah,
Even if your lips meet mine.

Though my touch may melt your skin,
Know that, your bones
Will not
Find a resting stop,
Here.

HOMECOMING

if you kiss.
and fondle. and touch this skin.
and this skin, does not
melt for you.
if, instead of cascading light
onto your every moon
you are met with the spine of a cold eclipse.
and this skin does not melt for you.
if you coax and tease and wait
jaw clenched, for honey to come,
and this skin
still does not melt
for you.
it is because
it is only, because,
this ancient skin
knows not to melt
for men
like
you.

- Wolves

to be loved. and not had.
therein lies the glory.

- Sweet Spot

HOMECOMING

for the men whose lines sizzle a little
on the flesh.
easy on the eyes,
chameleon hand round the waist.
truth, may elude them,
charm does not.
for the men whose shells are made out of steel
tell them,
arch tall, don't let them see your human.
tell them,
swallow the anger whole,
don't let them see you wince.
for the men who burrow into
crisp white sheets,
mumbling half-syllables to semi-strangers.
the only warmth they know is of bourbon
mixed with tongue.
for the men
who have made whole homes
out of the very skin which they roast over spitting fire..

if you wholly believe
to be more fragile flesh
makes you any less man..
tell em,
let it burn baby,
let it forever burn.

- Masculine

come in,
take off your angst
put down the weight,
the world is heavy love.
come in,
strip down to your eyes,
your essence, is all I see love.
come in,
pull down the blinds
unburden your limbs
recline.
I'm so glad you are here, love.

- Relief

HOMECOMING

I am a refugee in my own city.
home is elusive
temperamental,
uncertain.
so, I spend my nights
pining for the skies,
and my days
crawling the distance
to get
to
you.

- Mileage

Directions

to get out
from under, and over.
you must walk through.
always through.

Questions of Being

my home is not found in Constantinople.
smoke rings and burning halva,
tavla nights and raki straight to the stomach.
living off of dreams
as your only bread and water
this, is all you baba.

my home is not found in Constantinople.
balancing watermelon on bike,
calloused hands hiding
delicate spirit.
spilling words on leather-bound parchments
no-one will ever see.
taking ferries at midnight across, two continents.
that, is all you baba.

my home is not found in Constantinople.
glistening sweat on the upper lip
of the man who sells
candied almonds on the street corner.
hastily he accepts your generous currency
as you put him in a swift tangible ease.
you always preferred the pauper
to the noble, baba.

HOMECOMING

my home is not found, in Constantinople.
I, a female entity too foreign.
all English-speaking tongue and chest out.
entirely too proud, too full
to exist, in a place such as this.

my home is not found in Constantinople
though this city, lingers in my veins also.
I could not strip my self of this ancestry,
this middle-eastern, this toil, this blood,
even if I wanted to.
see,
the city and I may be strangers
reluctantly playing our roles.
though
because you are the sun in all my days,
though
because I was made in your image,
home is not found, in Constantinople.
but you,
are my eternal home, baba.

HOMECOMING

Eternal one,
You are my soft spot,
My softest spot
My very insides.
Delicate one,
You are the sliver in all my linings
The sunshine in my eyes,
I am forever blinded by you.
Loving one,
You are my water and my soil,
My reset, my nourishment.
Your skin is my skin.
Sweet one,
Your quiet elegance,
Has filled this soul
For damn over a decade.
I have been gifted
I have been granted,
Another self outside of self.
Oldest one,
The one I don't know how to be without,
Many have come and gone
But it is you, I could never replace.

- Soul Sister

A friend that knows your eyes.
your, every
kind of eyes.
What a divine offering,
What a sacred gift.

- Familiar

[II] the DROUGHT

HOMECOMING

HOMECOMING

II

name your pain.
call her, necessary
call her, heart-wrenching,
even call her, familiar.
just whatever you do,
do not call her
'home'.

there are sentences I still can't finish.
even after all these years.
even after all that these words
have done
for me.

- Honest

It was on the seventh, of the ninth month of the year.
A whole two months precariously early
At thirty minutes past midnight,
That you gave birth
To your first, and only daughter.
They named it Cerebral Palsy.
You named her, Başak.

- Virgo.

Your body carries the trauma so well
You almost forget
That confidence was pounded into you
From the moment that you were born.
Lip to breast,
It was the first thing mama ever gave you.
She knew it was,
The only thing, that could
Sustain you,
In a world this, indifferent.

- Sustenance

Brick and Mortar

Some nights I plead with the Universe
Turn me back into soil,
So that I may feed my soul.
Let me be one with the heartbeat of the Earth, again.

Only then,
Will I know rain to be
More nourishment which nurtures,
Then sorrow which drowns.

Practise the words you'll speak
Like Psalms to the head.
Memorise every curve,
Swallow every syllable.
Do this,
So you'll know what to say,
When they ask.

You know they'll ask.

- Eyes

I'm terrified that the ugly,
the dark,
the unspoken,
Will make its presence known.
So I fill these pages with my blood,
And wait for dawn to rise.

- Rituals

HOMECOMING

The moon,
She cries for me.
Wishing she could reflect
Some of her abundance back into the depths of my soul.
You cannot penetrate this flesh
Though many have tried.
You cannot sew the weight of worth back in.

- Luna

HOMECOMING

Hurts me to see,
For all of your insight,
You still do not see yourself
in.all.of.your.splendour.

- Blind

HOMECOMING

I will quietly,
gently,
pick every piece of myself up.
gather all that is broken, mismatched,
all that they could not see,
all that they were so quick to reject.
I will kiss
affirmations into every surface of this skin
so that my worth, my beauty stands whole.

I will start over
rebuild, this time with all that I've been given, not all I've been left.
like a grandmothers quilt, I will pluck from the very fabric of my tapestry
I will mould and craft,
so that my every eccentric colour
My every irregular shape
is but, one whole, of a beautiful trajectory,
all.its.own.

- Homecoming

HOMECOMING

When the pain overflows.
It stings, it scalds.
It threatens to scar, to mould, to define.
When your so full
Swimming in oceans of despair.
How depleted, how tormented.
Rear mirror tells you what you already know.
Soul lingers behind, dragging her feet.
Self-inflicted, perhaps,
Circumstantial, perhaps.
You've stopped giving a shit.
After all,
Unveiling the reason for the darkness.
Doesn't bring salvation
When nighttime comes.

- Real

I am a multitude of contradictions.
I have existed so my entire life.

- Tension

HOMECOMING

I think I
must exist
somewhere between
purgatory and salvation.
how else
do I explain
this constant mourn
of moons gone,
intertwined with,
an insatiable lust,
for what is to come?

I guess I'm yearning for,
all that I'm letting go of,
at the same damn time.

- Nostalgic

Sometimes understanding is not ours to taste.

- Hindsight

Hands that caress, but do not commit.
Lips that touch, but do not give in fully to the taste.
Addicted to that which is unattainable, unavailable,
This is it's own particular breed of masochism.

- The Yearn

Rumi's Field

Surely my sins
have found
yours?

some nights
the depths of my soul lie
parallel to my body.
detached, unacknowledged,
like a stranger at the door.

- Unknown

HOMECOMING

You can travel the entirety of the world,
Live and breathe in another continent,
Tiptoe into Irish bars on Bleecker
To hear that once familiar sound.
Go into basements you have no place being,
Just for a little resonance.

Only to come home
And find nothing that wants you,
Quite as badly, as you wanted it.

- Foreigner

HOMECOMING

I tried to capture my old breath,
my old lust with these new eyes.
banged on my own chest and listened as my screams sat
muffled amongst a city of lights.
I tried to wear my old thrill
rouge lipstick with a frozen smile,
put it on for size.

I searched this skin to feel for my old heart,
though she, had long left with the wind.
I slipped into this old flesh,
brimming it was, with past lovers once again.

I peeled back all these layers
In stinging tribute
to an old
and decayed life.
I did all of this in stark remembrance,
only ever for the night though,
only ever for the night.

- Convenient Amnesia

HOMECOMING

The curious thing about leaving
Is that you never come back
Quite the person you once were.
You may never be the same twice,
Though, nor is the adopted city, you left behind.

- Things They Don't Tell You

Maybe you and I are only ever meant to share the same sky.

- Musings II

HOMECOMING

If we only have this life,
may you find me, and pluck me
out from amongst
the thorns.

- Rose By Another Name

HOMECOMING

The rebuilding effort
Takes a village.
And it's almost always
After
He's had his way.
Why do I let him
Have his way?

- Tsunami

Forgive the sins that have transpired against this skin.
The ones you committed despite your best intentions.
Forgive yourself, for being a prisoner
To the potency of the well-placed word.

- Transgressions

HOMECOMING

Spiritual sustenance sought.

- PSA

HOMECOMING

tonight I burn for you
burn at the stake for you.
even though
succumbing
to you
into. you.
leaves me on my knees
every time.
long,
after,
you've,
gone.

- Sacrificial

Rooms

There should be a vacant sign
Hanging up above my bedpost
For all the nights I seem to spend alone.

Darling,
It is better that then,
To entangle your sheets
With the wrong kind of love
That's the worst kind of love.

Dam

I built castles in the sand which washed away with the tide.
If I ever learn patience, maybe we can build our own one day.

HOMECOMING

Mama taught me strength, as my first language.
Love came after.
No wonder I am so well versed in one,
and not the other.

- Armour

The Not Quite Love

And what do you say of those late night desires?
That burning that engulfs and stirs
Dark, deep, tantalising,
In all, the most sinful, of my crevices.
Lips parted,
A sharp intake of breath,
I reminisce.
Limbs tangled, soft secrets whispered into erect skin
At attention,
Burns inflicted
From a world of chaos and monotony.
You soothe the scalding,
Place balm over the hurt
You know, where it hurts.
Waters run deep
I am immersed,
Cascading down
Deeper below.
Refuge is found, here.
In the presence of the spirit,
I gather my craving
In the palm of my hand.
Sacrifices to the moon,
On the longest of nights.
Ode to the women
That I have become.
The women of silent yearnings.
I do this, as I remember you,
You.
A soft and hard place,
All at once.

HOMECOMING

I realise you are awake somewhere else and it
cuts through me.
kindness curdles in my mouth,
compassion does not know to visit.
hands outstretched, when it comes to you,
this blessing is not freely given.
this blessing is not freely given.
this blessing is not,
yours.

I realise you are sucking on another earlobe
and the taste of tongue strains my stomach.
muscles pull at the thought of you,
thighs touching, hand on thighs, thick and smoke filled eyes.
eyes that wander,
eyes that glaze,
over.

I realise you are resting into someone else's breast,
breathing breath into breast, sucking breast, head gently
rest, lullabies sing all that I could not be,
all that once was, and it trickles through me.

I realise I am living without you.

I realise you are living,
with, or without me.

- The Hold

HOMECOMING

I miss you on my quiet days.
With a certain, simmering passion.
If only I could throw my arms around your own
and breathe in your skin.

I only breathed in,
your skin after all.

- Home Away From Home

I have found,
like wine stains
on white tablecloth,
the imprint of you,
never fully fades.

so full of feeling
this soul has become,
If I was ever moved by you,
I will forever be moved by you.

Impressions

I have never known
eyes
for
life.

- Honest II

[III] the SPRING

HOMECOMING

HOMECOMING

That good good love.
That, baking banana bread in the kitchen, kind of love.
That, let's wear out these sheets, kind of love.
While Lauryn plays overhead kind of love.
Come home to me love.
Come home to me love.

Don't you know this body has been waiting for you?

- Housewife

HOMECOMING

it was a slow simmer
the way we,
fell into each other.

- Fusion

The taste of you is momentary.
Something you can't quite capture.
Like, the dance you see on a rainy city night,
Between the glistening pavements
And the golden street lights.

- Magic

That which cannot be gained.
I have spent a lifetime
trying to acquire you.

- **Love and Other Drugs**

Love looks so good on you love.
The way you wear it,
The way it clings to your wrists,
And drapes around your thighs.
Like wheat fields on a summer's day,
You sway effortlessly.
Weight suspended,
Skin forever basking in the sun.

- **Tanned**

HOMECOMING

The space we craft,
Does not need to stretch for miles.
It does not need to be adorned with velvet
Or thunder, to make its presence known.
Light may not reach into its every crevice
And some days the walls will stink with the kind of
neglect, you just can't scrub off.

The space we craft,
Does not need to feed off of others eyes to be
sustained.
We do not need,
Their heaving and breathing swirling like dust,
A weight of opinions left on the doorstep.

The space we craft,
Does not need to be woven through golden thread to be
deemed worthy.
Hands do not need to be clasped shimmering in the sun.
Fates do not need to be cemented by the stars.

The space we craft,
Needs to be in the here, and the now.
The space we craft, needs to be,
Only ever,
Only ever,
Only ever,
Ours.

- Sacred.

at the mention of your name
the Universe herself, pulsates.

(it is the purest thrill I have ever known).

- Tangible

the warmth
that draws you in.
that makes a home in the belly of your stomach.
it tells you all that you ever need to know.
every,
single,
time.

- Intuition

HOMECOMING

my intuition sweet talkin' me again.
no baby, please baby.
don't go there again.

I know I know.
there's just something
in those eyes,
I could never resist.

- Vice

my love for you is an ever expanding ocean.
just when I think I can't,
there you go again.
making me free fall,
making me
crash back into your depths.

- Submerged

HOMECOMING

Like sweet molasses
clinging to the gums.
few things
stop me in my tracks like
the sight of you.

The chemicals react and I,
taste the audacity you inspire
travelling up my spine.
What utter chaos you cause,
What delightful, rapture.

- Chemistry

It took all this unravelling,
All this undressing,
To strip down to the core.
My own full, naked reflection,
Mirrored against
The river of your warm gaze.
It took all of this
Outpouring,
To feel, to find.
Something which cannot be
Explained.
It took all of this unbecoming,
To give in to
A moment captured.
The kind of connection which can only be replayed,
Never replicated.

- Final Call

HOMECOMING

Don't you know love,
It is you love,
It has always been you love.

- Chosen

I bite.
and you drip down my chin.
the kind of succulence
I could get addicted to.

- Lips

HOMECOMING

I have felt my way through you.
in your absence,
raw knuckles to chest.
pleading for salvation,
for end,
for void,
for something
final.
for something
absolute.

I have felt my way through you.
the sheer kindness in your eyes,
the depth of your tone,
stops my breath.
breath-less.
I stand.
even now, even still.

I have felt my way through you.
reeling yet giddy
at the thought,
drawn to that honey-suckled drawl
that you wear so well.
I have felt my way through you,
touched,
and coaxed,
and inspected,
every surface of this body

to see,
to feel,
where you entered through.

I have felt my way through you.
and somehow,
some way,
you ended up
on the inside of my insides,
looking out,
at me.

- Stomach

HOMECOMING

You have your mother's thick hair,
Her uncanny persuasion,
Her almond eyes.
Most of all however,
You have the anchor of her presence.
Just like her,
They know when you enter a room,
And they feel it,

Always feel it,

 When you leave.

- Palatable

With ease, or not at all.

- Mantra

HOMECOMING

Things To Come

there are lessons I've yet to learn.
pending truths,
I taste them, on my tongue.
fist to jaw,
I fear their weight.
the impact, leaves me
stinging,
reeling,
bleeding,
already.
though the first hit,
hasn't even come to pass.

the intuition is near prophetic.
so I'm reminded of all the things
I've stomached,
and all the things, I've yet too.

like,
how I can't sit still under your burning gaze
you had to ask if you could stare.
or how I can't stand cramped spaces or uncomfortable
conversations.
so I replicate the same temporary longings,
and then despair at the empty spaces between my fingers.

HOMECOMING

see,
I already know,
when you
finally find me.
in this lifetime.
I will scratch and scream, hell bent on
destruction.

oh, revolutionary spirit,
will you ever know how to build
with both brick, and mortar?
or will you forever chase the wind
letting the sand of potential, slip from your fingers?

HOMECOMING

so accustomed I have become,
to, that-which-does-not resonate
that I can never quite recognise,
that-which-does.

- Cold

HOMECOMING

rations of soul,
sustain me.
those that are
left in,
the cracks.
those that are,
found in between
teeth, in gesture, in touch, in warmth, in tongue, in kiss, in
embrace, in hurt, in melody, in speech, in sex, in spirit.

This is the source of my energy.
This is the reason for my breath.

- Mouth to Mouth

HOMECOMING

For Your Eyez

one day.
I will peel off these clothes just, like, this.
till I lay there in
nothing,
but
skin.

and we will make,
a movie out of our bodies.

HOMECOMING

Memories

melting into you.
that is all I recall.

Let's take that rare, sacred journey,
to a dimension only our spirits know.
Let's lay bare our bodies,
so that we may be granted
the kind of carnal knowledge
that lets our souls fly.
Let's make the kind of love
which permeates the flesh,
which burns us into ash,
which
utterly,
completely,
and totally,
exhausts our angels.

- Intimate

HOMECOMING

Certain

if you believe in nothing else, believe this.
all things are
delicately
and
deliciously,
interconnected.

look what I did baby.
look what you made me do.
the love that lives in the sky
I put it all in these pages.
look baby,
read baby,
I wrote all that I could never say.

- Communication

HOMECOMING

the sentiments were so pure, and fluid,
they tumbled down my fingers like velvet.
I made love to the page so naturally.
forgive me.
I didn't even realise,
I wrote about you.
I've been writing about you.

You,
are all I know what to write about.

- Muse

[IV] the BLOOM

HOMECOMING

HOMECOMING

My first love,
My kindred spirit,
My second heart.
You have been, and will continue to be,
My twin soul.
For as long as I hold breath in my lungs.
Of this, and only this,
I am irrevocably sure.

- Baba

Though you were birthed in water,
You were built, in the fire.
Don't let your resilience burn, you.
Remain malleable clay for
Every hardened heart you encounter.

The journey to self, is forever upstream.
And you must allow yourself to be
Moulded and crafted,
By the same water, from which, you were formed.
If you hope to ever, swim your way back home.

- Shapes

I keep pulling at the roots,
Bring it into existence.
Speak on him.
Let the honey drip from your tongue,
Sickly sweet.
Speak on him.
If only to,
Bring him to the surface of my mind.
Speak on him.
If only to,
Feel how deep,
I speak on him.
How embedded he is,
Within the tapestry of me,
I speak on him.
And still,
I have never been able to,
Unearth the size of him,
From within,
From out under,
the depths of me.

- Planted

I wish to immortalise you,
I wish to salvage you.
If only in the depths of my memory.
If only in the words on these pages.

- Ingrained

Naked

How can this sacred ritual,
Of putting pen to paper.
An act, as timeless, as the lunar tides,
Burn and soothe, so deliciously?
Uncover and undress so much?

HOMECOMING

Practise being soft.
Cloak yourself in warm words.
Embrace the shadows in your flesh.
Make love, often
And then, only in candlelight.
Do this, on the days that you need reminding.
Your tongue need not remain sharp, eternally.
Soft, is strong, too.

- Allowances

HOMECOMING

Quietly I confront the morning light.
It is still, now.
The darkness no longer consumes.

- Dawn

HOMECOMING

Baby girl,
You,
Were the only thing you ever needed.

- Sufficient

HOMECOMING

it is a practised art, this.
years of appearing as one thing,
and actually existing as another.
guess it's the only way I know how to protect
that most sacred of energy,
guess it's the only way these depths can remain,
untainted.

- Introvert

This journey into self-mastery, into self,
Is not pleasant, or even comfortable.
It is all jagged edge and biting lip.
It is skin grazed by the steeliness of the thing,
The thing you cannot feel.
The thing you will not consume,
To be true.
This journey into self-mastery, into self
Is not comfortable, or even pleasant.
But oh is it necessary,
Oh is it necessary.

- Trajectories

HOMECOMING

I wonder if,
We will ever be iconised
In this lifetime.
For writing about,
The Same Old Shit.
In different light.

- ~~Young Kings~~

HOMECOMING

the journey
is
within.
in every conceivable way.

- Layers

HOMECOMING

I was convinced from a young age
if I scoured every inch of this mental,
learnt every motivation behind this heart,
no one could meet me,
and tell me,
something about me,
that I did not already know.
then you came
and I,
met me,
all over,
and over, and over again.

- Waves

my purpose is of a language
that can spin the broken with the gold.
that can heal the splinters born
from the emotional carnage,
that comes with the daily business of
sanctimonious living.

if I can offer up
my hurt, for your eyes.
pieces of soul, on brass platter
to digest at your choosing.
if I choose to shed,
these most familial of shackles.

know that there is salvation in this process
know that for every dark night fall.
there is a city of lights.
and know that
it is within the light where freedom,
lives.

- Kintsugi

HOMECOMING

peel off your clothes.
take off the day.
let it all fall into a heap by the chequered tiles.
stand naked under the warm water.
let the water,
run.
scoop a handful of eucalyptus oil.
rubbing the shoulders first,
then the neck,
then the breasts,
travel your own hands
down your own torso.
reach into the small of your back.
reach into, all of the places
his hands once made home.

allow yourself a small mercy;
remember all the parts of you
that once softened at his touch.
know that your skin may never soften
quite like that again.
this is a fact.
make peace, with this fact.

re-introduce yourself to yourself.
make pleasantries, with your thighs.
taking the warm water, in circular motion,
allow yourself to be drenched.

breathe in, as you see the dirt
mix with the residue.
watch as it swirls into the drain.
make sure, it swirls into the drain.

breathe out.
scrub, harder.
pray for this new skin.
whisper to the sky:
you must forget,
you must forget.

try to mean it, this time.

'Shedding'

the one I pined for.
scratched dirt, under nail for.
changed shape for.
grasped in my hurt for.

could never match
the one,
that I,
was actually made
for.

- Fit

the energy you hold,
is the kind which cannot be replicated.
make no mistake.
it is the very thing,
which brings them back,
every.
single.
time.

- Authentic

these gentle waters,
can turn into rippling waves
instantly, and without,
warning.
if you do not learn how to swim,
you will drown within the depths of my mind.

- Intense

HOMECOMING

I am a daughter of Eve.
untangle me,
unearth me.
uproot, me.

I am a daughter of Eve.
dismantle me,
pleasure me.
give into, me.

I am a daughter of Eve.
and though there maybe no mercy
in a creation such as this.
there will be no shame either.
there will be no shame, *ever*.

- Sexual

we shape so much of our feminine,
so much of our female,
after the male gaze.
so much of our motion,
so much of our hips,
after the male desire.
live and die,
and tuck and pull,
to make a man, desire.
the things we do,
the skin we rouse,
to make a man, desire.

fuck that breed
of male desire.
the kind that demands you
offer anatomy up in gratitude.
the kind that meets bare neck with teeth.
the kind whose eyes can never be fed.

I would rather have.
I would rather know.
do you sister,
drip wet.
pine for.
desire after,
yourself?

- Hunger

the weight.
of my words.
would sink you.
should I choose, to speak them.

-Silent.

HOMECOMING

I am.
home to myself.
In this body,
I have long since cultivated.
In this body,
I have long since rejected.
I sit here, in utter solitude with nothing but silence for company.
and wonder, is this what it is to be?

HOMECOMING

I am convinced that heaven is within the spaces in the sky.
will I ever have space?
to call my own,
to call my home.
will I ever share space?
will the gaps between my fingers interlock with your own
to form, that most sacred of space?

- Musings

HOMECOMING

Do not give in.
Do you hear me?
Even when you are drowning,
Unable to birth full sentences
Foaming at the mouth.
Your own hand,
Clasped around,
Your own neck.

Do not give in.
Even when,
The night sky consumes you,
And moonlight does not know to visit.

Do not give in.
Even when you think solitude
Is the only body,
You will ever inhibit.

There exists a place
Beyond the dark,
Out yonder.
Do not give in,
The Light will find you,
The Light will carry you home.

- Solo

perhaps this is the hardest task of all.
to write on that
which has been brewing in the dark.
it scalds so deeply.
and yet,
you must bring it to the surface.
you must air out, the windows of your pain.
if you ever hope
to be,
free.

perhaps this is the hardest, ask of all.
that in order to,
set yourself free.
you must first,
knowingly,
necessarily,
set yourself,
on fire.

- Darkest Before Dawn

HOMECOMING

I wonder when you talk of me,
if honey drips from your tongue.
or if.
your nose crinkles.
eyes water.
mouth still trying to rid yourself of the taste.

- Sour

HOMECOMING

you don't know
all of the others
made up the parts
were segments
were understudies
were substitutes
of the whole
pure feeling
that I
found
in
you.

- Replacement

HOMECOMING

How many versions of ourselves
must we shape shift into,
in order to find the one that feels right?

How many different lifetimes
must we live before we,
settle into the one,
that hugs our contours?

Will we ever reach the life that fits like a glove?
Is there such a thing?

- Questions

HOMECOMING

I belong to me.
Know this to be the highest of truths.
And if you ever need reminding?

(Ink it on your fucking skin).

- Answers

HOMECOMING

We write.
Because the words that come to us,
Must come through us.
Make no mistake,
All these letters are my offspring.
All this ink is, my blood.

- Children

these hands which I bathe with,
and cook with,
and tend to you with,
and sex with,
and caress with.
they have been both brick and water.
they have carried both love and loss.
these hands which I express with,
and create with,
and write with.
they are,
and always will be,
the gunpowder
in my rifle.
they are,
and always will be,
My last, defining, shot.

- Leftie.

HOMECOMING

there are any number of things I could tell you.

I could tell you that there are exactly 7 ways Browning
counts love in Sonnet 43.
I could tell you whether or not two people have slept
together by the inclination of their bodies.
I could tell you that Corinthians 13 is the only bible verse
I've ever committed to memory.
It is the only one I care to
remember.

I could tell you the amount of years
that you've been on this earth,
or that we all long for the warmth of the womb
from the moment that we leave it.
I could tell you that in order to thrive in this life,
you need to be both brave and bold, in equal measure.

I could tell you that there are a thousand different ways a
women can reach pleasure, if done right.

That hands really do heal.
That you should only ever drink doubles.
That you should always, *always* let it burn.

there are any number I could not tell you.

I could not tell you the circumference of the sun,
or her distance from the moon.
I could not tell you why we run through our entire lives.
I could not tell you where we are all trying to go.
I could not tell you why they killed Emmett Till,
or who committed such a heinous act.
I could not tell you why I never learnt the piano,
though my fingers crave still, to glide over the keys.
I cannot tell you why we allow all that we do not say
to linger in the air,
like fruit gone rotten.

I cannot tell you why we look for truths
in between the folds of another's skin.
I cannot tell you where the guiding light comes from,
or where it goes when it leaves.

I could not tell you
all of the things,
that I do not know.
Like, how I loved you.

Like, how you were not allowed to stay.

Birthright

may I always
overflow,
in golden splendour,
like those dancing fields of gold.
may I always dare to own
all of this
abundance.
the very kind
that envelops my flesh.
the very kind
 that is in my name.

HOMECOMING

Sister.
You are at your most beautiful
When your eyes are inflamed,
When your soul is enraptured,
When you speak your truth,
And align with the rhythm of your heartbeat.

Shine baby, shine.

Passionate is *forever* sexy.

- Never Forget

the prayers you pray
to the whimsical skies,
when you slip into something good.
the embrace of you smoulders
with a kind of old intimacy
that reverberates within my very bones.

I know you.

I've known you,
my whole life.

- The Knowledge

Equilibrium

I flow into various states of being so often.
the weight of the years,
sinking like sediment,
swirling like sand grains beside my ankles.

It is time now, to begin anew.
slip on garments of silk.
bathe in rosewater.
press only love, into every surface of this skin.

we are not perfectly formed, not any of us.
so tonight,
I will whisper to my angels.
find delight in every curve,
and give thanks for my specific blend
of womanhood.

for this amalgamation.
for this sweet, conscientious spirit.

HOMECOMING

♥

Printed in Poland
by Amazon Fulfillment
Poland Sp. z o.o., Wrocław